Let's find out about

Jesus

Stephanie Jeffs
and Jenny Tulip

Contents

Baby Jesus

Things Jesus Did

People Jesus Met

Stories Jesus Told

Bible stories can be found as follows:

Mary and the angel: Luke 1:26-38

The journey to Bethlehem: Luke 2:1-5

No room at the inn: Luke 2:6-7

Baby Jesus: Luke 2:6-7

Shepherds and angels: Luke 2:8-12

Angels everywhere: Luke 2:13-15

The shepherds find the baby: Luke 2:16-20

Wise men see a new star: Matthew 2:1

A visit to the palace: Matthew 2:2-8

The wise men find Jesus: Matthew 2:9-12

Baby Jesus

Mary and the angel

One day, the angel Gabriel came to earth.
He had a wonderful message from God.

Mary was afraid when she saw the angel.

'Don't be frightened,' said Gabriel.
'God is very pleased with you.
You are going to have a special baby.
He will be God's own Son.'

Mary loved God very much.
She wanted to obey him.
'I will do whatever God wants,' she said.

Where was Mary when she was surprised by
the angel?

The journey to Bethlehem

Mary and Joseph lived in Nazareth.
Joseph was a carpenter.
They were going to get married.

The Emperor wanted to count the people.
'Everyone must go to their family town,' he said.
So Mary and Joseph had to go to Bethlehem.
It was a long journey.

Mary was excited.
She would soon have God's special baby.

How did Mary and Joseph get to Bethlehem?

No room at the inn

Bethlehem was very busy.
Lots of other people had gone there too.

Mary was very tired.
She knew that her baby would soon be born.
She wanted to rest.

Mary and Joseph stopped at the inn.
'Have you anywhere to sleep?' Joseph asked.
The innkeeper shook his head.
The inn was full.

A kind man saw how tired Mary was.
'You can sleep in my stable,' he said.

How many people can you see inside the inn?

Baby Jesus

Mary and Joseph went into the stable.
Everything was quiet.

After a while, Mary's baby was born.
She wrapped him in strips of cloth.
Then she made a bed for him in the manger.

Mary and Joseph watched the baby.
'His name is Jesus,' said Joseph.

Why was the manger filled with hay?

Shepherds and angels

In the fields near Bethlehem,
some shepherds were looking after their sheep.

It was night-time, and everything was dark.
Suddenly they saw a bright light!
It was an angel, sent by God.
They were frightened.

'Don't be afraid!' said the angel.
'I have some wonderful news.
Tonight a very special baby has been born.
He is wrapped in strips of cloth.
He is lying in a manger.
He is God's gift for the whole world!'

Can you see how the shepherds were keeping warm?

Angels everywhere

Suddenly the sky was full of angels.
'Glory to God!' they sang. 'Peace on earth.'

The shepherds were amazed.
They had never seen anything like it!

When the angels had gone, they said,
'Let's go and find this special baby!'

They left their sheep and ran down the hillside
to Bethlehem.

Count the shepherds' crooks.

The shepherds find the baby

At last they came to the stable.
When they saw baby Jesus lying in the manger,
they knew they had found the right place.

They told Mary and Joseph about the angels.
'This baby is very special,' they said.

The shepherds left the stable.
They were so excited they told everyone,
'A wonderful thing has happened tonight!'

Find the shepherd who is carrying a lamb.

Wise men see a new star

Far, far away, some wise men saw a new star.
It shone brightly in the night sky.

'Whatever does it mean?' they asked.
They looked in their scrolls.
They searched through their charts.

'A new king has been born!' they said.
'Let's go and find him.'

So the wise men followed the star.
They wanted to worship the new king.

Find the new star shining in the sky.

A visit to the palace

At last the wise men reached Jerusalem.
They went to see King Herod in his palace.

'We have come to find the new king,' they said.
'We want to worship him.'

Herod knew nothing about a new king.
He was cross. He did not want a new king.
He asked his helpers to find out more.

Then he told the wise men, 'Go to Bethlehem.
Tell me where you find the new king.
I would like to see him too.'

Which one is King Herod?

The wise men find Jesus

The wise men followed the bright star,
until they came to a house in Bethlehem.

They found baby Jesus with his mother, Mary.

The wise men knelt down before Jesus.
They gave the baby king gifts:
gold, frankincense and myrrh.

They did not tell Herod that they had found Jesus,
but they went home another way.

Point to the gifts the wise men have brought.

Bible stories can be found as follows:

Jesus was baptised: Matthew 3:13-17

Jesus went to a wedding: John 2:1-11

The huge catch of fish: Luke 5:1-11

Jesus taught his friends how to pray: Matthew 6:7-13

The very big picnic: John 6:1-15

Jesus went to Matthew's party: Matthew 9:9-13

Jesus made a blind man see: Mark 8:22-26

Jesus helped a man to walk: John 5:1-9

Jesus calmed a storm: Luke 8:22-25

Jesus rode on a donkey: Matthew 21:1-11

Things Jesus Did

Jesus was baptised

One day Jesus went to the River Jordan.
He saw John by the river.
John had a message from God.
'Come and be washed in the water,' said John.
'Get ready for God's new life!'

Many people came to be baptised.
They were washed in the river.

But when Jesus came to be baptised,
John was surprised.
He knew that Jesus was special.

When Jesus came out of the water,
God's voice from heaven said,
'This is my Son. I love him.'

Find the dove flying in the air.

Jesus went to a wedding

Everywhere Jesus went, things happened.
One day, Jesus was invited to a wedding.
Everyone was happy.
There was plenty to eat and drink.

Jesus' friends were with him.
His mother Mary was there too.
Suddenly Mary saw that all the wine had gone!
She asked Jesus to help.
Jesus spoke to the servants.
'Fill those pots with water,' he said.

When the servants poured out the water,
it had changed into delicious wine.
Then Jesus' friends realised he was special.

Can you find six water pots?

The huge catch of fish

One day Jesus was by Lake Galilee.
Many people came to hear him talk about God.
Jesus sat in Peter's boat to talk to the people.

Later, they went out on the lake.
Jesus said to Peter, 'Let down your nets.'
'We fished all night,' replied Peter and Andrew.
'But we caught nothing.'

Because Jesus said so, Peter let down his nets.
Suddenly the nets were full of fish!
The nets began to break.
James and John came to help in their boat.
They were all amazed.
'Come with me,' said Jesus.
So they left their boats to follow him.

How many fishermen followed Jesus?

Jesus taught his friends how to pray

One day Jesus talked to his friends about God.
'Teach us what to say to him,' they asked.
So Jesus taught them how to pray.

'God is like a good father,' said Jesus.
'He knows what you need before you ask.
But pray like this:'

'Our Father in heaven.
Your name is special and holy.
May your kingdom come quickly.
May we do good things each day where we live,
just like in heaven.
Please give us everything we need each day.
Forgive us when we do things wrong.
Help us to forgive other people, too.'

Find the little lamb with its mother.

The very big picnic

Lots of people came to listen to Jesus.
It was late, and they were hungry.
'We must feed all these people,' said Jesus.

Jesus' friends had no food.
They did not know what to do.
Then Andrew found a boy with a picnic lunch.
He had five rolls and two fish.

Jesus took the boy's food.
He said thank you to God.
Then he shared the food with all the people.
Everyone had enough to eat.

'Collect what is left over,' said Jesus.
His friends put all that was left into baskets.

How many baskets can you see?

Jesus went to Matthew's party

One day Jesus met a man called Matthew.
Matthew wanted to be Jesus' friend.
Lots of people didn't like Matthew,
because Matthew was a tax collector.
He collected money for the Romans.
Sometimes he cheated and took too much.

Matthew had a special party for Jesus.
He invited all his friends to come to his house.
Lots of them were tax collectors too.
Jesus cared about them.
He wanted to be with them.

When Matthew met Jesus he left his job.
He stopped cheating people.
He began to do good things.
He became a friend of Jesus.

What food did the people at the party eat?

Jesus made a blind man see

Jesus met a blind man in a village by the lake.
The man's friends brought him to Jesus.
'Jesus, make him see,' they begged.

So Jesus took the man out of the village.
He put some spit on the man's eyes.
'Can you see?' asked Jesus.

'Yes, I can see!' said the man.
'But the people look like trees walking about.'

So Jesus put his hands on the man's eyes.
Then the man could see everything clearly.
'Thank you, Jesus,' he said.

Find a bunch of grapes. What colour are they?

Jesus helped a man to walk

One day when Jesus was in Jerusalem,
he saw a man who could not walk.
The man was lying on a mat by a pool.
Many people came to the pool every day.
They thought the water could make them better.

'Do you want to get better?' Jesus asked him.
'Yes, I do,' said the man.
'Then get up,' said Jesus.
'Pick up your mat and walk.'

The man trusted Jesus.
He picked up his mat and began to walk!
Everyone was amazed.
'Who can Jesus be?' they asked themselves.

Point to the steps going down into the pool.

Jesus calmed a storm

It was the end of a very busy day.
'Let's sail across the lake!' said Jesus.
So Jesus and his friends jumped into a boat.

Jesus was very tired and soon fell fast asleep.
Suddenly the wind began to howl.
The waves began to roll.
The little boat rocked up and down.
'Help!' cried Jesus' friends.

Jesus stood up. 'Quiet!' he said to the wind.
'Be still!' he said to the waves.
Immediately everything was calm.

'Jesus is very special,' whispered his friends.
'Even the wind and the waves do what he says.'

How many boats are on the lake?

Jesus rode on a donkey

Jesus and his friends were going to Jerusalem.
They were walking along the road.

'Bring me a donkey,' said Jesus.
'You'll find one waiting in the next village.'
So Jesus' friends found the donkey.
They brought it to Jesus.

Jesus rode on the donkey into the city.
Lots of people stood beside the road.
They saw Jesus riding the donkey.
They flung their cloaks on to the ground.
They pulled palm branches from the trees.
They waved them in the air.
'Hosanna!' they cried.
'Here comes King Jesus!'

How many palm branches can you see?

Bible stories can be found as follows:

Jesus and his friends: Mark 1:16-20; Mark 2:13-17

The friends who helped: Mark 2:1-12

Jesus and the Roman soldier: Matthew 8:5-13

Jesus heals a little girl: Mark 5:21-42

Jesus and the two sisters: Luke 10:38-42

The very rich man: Mark 10:17-31

The ten men on the road: Luke 17:11-19

Jesus meets Bartimaeus: Mark 10:46-52

The little tax collector: Luke 19:1-9

Jesus and the little children: Mark 10:13-16

People Jesus Met

Jesus and his friends

'Follow me,' called Jesus.
'Help me tell everyone about God.'

Simon and Andrew were fishermen.
They left their nets by Lake Galilee.

James and John left their boats.

Matthew, the tax collector, left his job.
Philip, Bartholomew, Thomas, James,
Simon, Judas and Judas Iscariot –
all decided to follow Jesus.

They became Jesus' special friends.

How many special friends did Jesus have?

The friends who helped

Once there was a man who couldn't walk.
He was so ill he couldn't move at all.
His friends carried him to Jesus.

The house was full of people.
So the friends carried the man on to the roof.
Then they made a hole in the roof and
let the man down to Jesus.

When Jesus saw the man he said,
'You can get up and go home!'
Jesus had made the man well!
The man got up and walked out of the house.
Everyone was amazed and thanked God.

Point to the man's friends.

Jesus and the Roman soldier

One day a Roman soldier came to Jesus.
'Please help me, Jesus,' he said.
'My dear servant is very ill in bed.'

'I will go and make him better,' promised Jesus.

'No,' said the soldier. 'You do not need to come to my house.
Just say so, and he will be better.'

Jesus was surprised.
'You are a good man of faith,' he said.
'Go home, and your servant will be better.'
The Roman soldier went home very happy
and found his dear servant completely well.

How many Roman soldiers can you see?

Jesus heals a little girl

Jairus was a very important man.
He rushed through the crowd, looking for Jesus.

'Please come to my house,' he begged.
'My little girl is very ill.'
But when Jesus reached the house,
the little girl had died.

Jesus went inside with Peter, James and John.
He held the little girl's hand.
'Little girl, get up now,' he said.

The little girl stood up.
Jesus had made her well again!

Find Jesus and the little girl.

Jesus and the two sisters

Mary and Martha were very excited.
Jesus and his friends were coming to stay.
There was so much to get ready!

Martha was still busy when Jesus arrived.
But Mary didn't do anything to help!
She sat and listened to Jesus.

Martha was cross. 'It's not fair!' she said.
'Tell Mary to help me.'

'Martha,' said Jesus kindly.
'Mary is doing the right thing.
Let's be together while we can.'

What food can you see on the table?

The very rich man

One day a rich man came to see Jesus.
'Tell me how I can please God,' he said.

'Obey him,' replied Jesus.
'I have done that,' said the man.
'There's one thing more,' said Jesus.
'Give away all your money.
Come with me to tell people about God.'

The man was sad. He was very, very rich.
He walked away from Jesus and went home.
Jesus was sad too.
He knew the man loved his money more than God.

What is the man wearing that shows he is rich?

The ten men on the road

Jesus was going to Jerusalem with his friends.
On the road he met ten men.
They had an illness which made their skin sore.
Nobody wanted to be with them.

'Jesus, help us! Make us better!' they shouted.

'Walk to the village and you will be better,' said Jesus.

The men walked to the village and when they got there,
they were all better.
One of them ran back to Jesus straight away.
'Thank you, Jesus!' he said.

Where are the nine men who forgot to say
thank you?

Jesus meets Bartimaeus

Bartimaeus was blind.
One day he heard that Jesus was coming.

'Jesus, help me!' he called.
'Be quiet!' someone shouted back unkindly.
But Jesus heard Bartimaeus.
'Come here!' he said.

Bartimaeus stood up and felt his way to Jesus.
'How can I help you?' asked Jesus.
'I know you can make me see,' said Bartimaeus.

Straight away Bartimaeus could see.
He followed Jesus joyfully.

Can you find the cloak, begging bowl and stick which
Bartimaeus has dropped on the ground?

The little tax collector

One day crowds of people came to see Jesus.
Zacchaeus was too small to see anything,
so he climbed a fig tree.

No one liked Zacchaeus.
He was rich because he cheated people
when he collected the taxes.

'Come down,' said Jesus.
'I'm staying at your house today.'

After that, Zacchaeus stopped cheating.
He gave back the money he had taken.
He became a friend of Jesus.

Find three people standing on the roofs
of their houses.

Jesus and the little children

Jesus' friends were fed up.
Crowds of people had brought their children
to see Jesus.

'Go away!' said Jesus' friends crossly.

'You mustn't say that!' said Jesus.
'I want the children to come to me.
God loves every single one of them.'

The children ran to Jesus.
He picked them up and blessed them.
Jesus loved the children, and they loved him.

Which toys can you see in the picture?

Bible stories can be found as follows:

God cares for you: Matthew 6:25-34

The two houses: Matthew 7:24-27

The perfect pearl: Matthew 13:45-46

The lost sheep: Matthew 18:12-14

The king's servant: Matthew 18:21-35

The good neighbour: Luke 10:30-37

The rich fool: Luke 12:16-21

The friend at midnight: Luke 11:5-10

The woman who lost a coin: Luke 15:8-10

The lost son: Luke 15:11-32

Stories Jesus Told

God cares for you

One day Jesus went up a hill with his friends.
He sat down to talk to them about God.

'You don't need to worry,' said Jesus.
'Look at the birds.
They have enough to eat and drink.
God looks after them, and he will look after you.'

'Look at the flowers,' said Jesus.
'God looks after them, and he will look after you.'

'God is like a good father.
He looks after us, and we are his children.'

How many birds are in the nest?

The two houses

Jesus told his friends a story about two houses.

'One day a man started to build a house.
He was sensible and he built his house on rock.
It was hard work,' said Jesus.

'Another man started to build a house.
He was lazy and he built his house on sand.
It was easy and did not take long.'

'But then the wind blew and the rain fell.
The lazy man's house came down with a crash.
But the sensible man's house was safe.'

'Listen carefully and do what I say,' said Jesus.
'Then you will be like the first man,
safe and sound.'

Where is the lazy man's goat? What is it doing?

The perfect pearl

'There was once a man,' said Jesus,
'who bought and sold pearls.'

'He looked everywhere for them.
He went to the market.
He went to the sea shore.
He looked at every pearl he could find.'

'Then one day he found a perfect pearl.
It was beautiful and it was expensive.
But the man knew what he had to do.
He sold everything he had.
Then he went to buy that pearl.'

'Following God is like that,' said Jesus.
'It is the most important thing to do.'

What is the man selling so that he can buy the pearl?

The lost sheep

'Once upon a time there was a shepherd,'
said Jesus, 'who had one hundred sheep.'

'Every day he counted his sheep.
One day he had only ninety-nine.
One was missing!'

'The shepherd left his other sheep.
He went to look for the lost one.
He looked everywhere until he found her.
Then he gently carried her home.
He was very happy – and so was the sheep.'

'God is like the shepherd,' said Jesus.
'He is always looking for us.
And he is very happy when we come back to him.'

Where are the shepherd's other sheep?

The king's servant

There was once a king who had a servant.
The servant owed him lots of money.
But the servant could not pay it back.

'Take him to prison!' shouted the king.
'Wait, I'll do my best to pay you back,'
said the servant on his knees.
The king was kind and forgave him.
And the servant went away happy.

But then the servant met another servant.
That servant owed him a little bit of money.
'Take him to prison!' shouted the first servant.
'Wait, I'll do my best to pay you back,'
said the second servant on his knees.
But he was flung into prison.

The king was angry when he heard this.
'I forgave you,' he said.
'You should forgive other people.'

Find the king's throne.

The good neighbour

'Be kind to other people,' said Jesus.
'Love your neighbour as you love yourself.'

'Who is my neighbour?' asked someone.
So Jesus told this story.

'There was once a man on a journey.
Suddenly some robbers jumped out at him.
They took his things and beat him up.'

'Nobody wanted to help the man.
Two people walked past without even stopping.
But along came a man from a different country.
He saw the man and felt sorry for him.
He looked after him and took him to an inn
so that he could get better.'

'That man was the good neighbour,' said Jesus.

Point to the good neighbour.

The rich fool

There was once a very rich man.
He had everything he could want.
He owned some land, and some barns.
Soon his barns were too small for all his grain.

'I'm rich,' he said.
'Now I will build myself bigger barns.
Then I can eat and drink and spend money
and I will be the happiest man in the world.'

But God spoke to the man.
'You are a fool,' said God. 'Tonight you will die.
Then who will enjoy all your riches? Not you!'

'Don't be greedy,' said Jesus.
'There is more to life than making money.'

What animals can you see on the farm?

The friend at midnight

'God is good and kind,' said Jesus.
'Ask him, and he will give you what you need.
Let me tell you a story about asking.'

'Late one night there was a knock at the door.
The family in the house were all asleep in bed.
"It's me, your friend!" called a voice from outside.
"What do you want?" shouted the father from his bed.'

'"A friend of mine has arrived," the voice replied.
"I have no food. Please give me some bread."
"Don't bother me," said the man in bed.
"The door is locked and we're all asleep."'

'But the friend knocked on the door again.
So at midnight the father of the house came down.
He gave his friend some bread.'

'Don't give up,' said Jesus. 'Keep on asking.'

Find the moon.

The woman who lost a coin

'God loves each one of you,' said Jesus.
'Let me tell you how much he loves you.'

'There was once a woman
who had ten silver coins,' said Jesus.
'One day one of her coins was missing!
So the woman lit a lamp and took a brush.
She swept the house from top to bottom.
She kept looking until she found the coin.'

'She was so happy. She told all her friends.
"Let's have a party! I've found my lost coin!"'

'God is like that.
He loves people so much that he doesn't give up
until they are safe in his care.'

What did the woman use to sweep her house?

The lost son

Jesus told a story about how much God loves us.

'There was once a young man.
He asked his father for money.
Then he went away to another country.
He spent all his money enjoying himself.
Soon he ran out of money.
He found a job, looking after pigs.
He was so hungry that even pig-food looked tasty!'

'The young man decided to go back home.
"I'll go and ask my father if I can be his servant."'

'At home, his father was waiting for him.
He ran to meet him. He hugged and kissed him.
"I've been a bad son," said the young man.
"Treat me like a servant!"
"You're my son!" said the father.
"Let's have a party.
I'm so happy to have you back home!"'

Find the new coat the father will give to his son.

Published in the UK by
The Bible Reading Fellowship
First Floor, Elsfield Hall, 15-17 Elsfield Way, Oxford OX2 8FG
ISBN 1 84101 404 4

This edition copyright © 2004 AD Publishing Services Ltd
1 Churchgates, The Wilderness, Berkhamsted, Herts HP4 2UB
Text copyright © 2000 AD Publishing Services Ltd, Stephanie Jeffs
Illustrations copyright © 2000 Jenny Tulip

Originally published in four volumes under the titles:
Baby Jesus
Things Jesus Did
People Jesus Met
Stories Jesus Told

Editorial Director Annette Reynolds
Design Krystyna Hewitt
Production John Laister

Printed and bound in Spain